I0621341

# Romar Press

Stephenville, Texas

2022

ISBN-13: 979-8-9853609-3-6

First Edition

FOR OENOPHILES EVERYWHERE
*especially Charles Robitaille*

# Wine Poems

# Marilyn Robitaille

## *Preface*

I hope you find this collection of poems and their accompanying photographs enjoyable. Pour yourself a glass of wine and take a look around. You'll find a good dose of humor, a little angst, and many heartfelt memories shared, all of them triggered by the poets' associations with wine. The poets are as varied as the poems' perspectives. They come three countries: Canada, England, and the U.S. We have representation from California to New York and points in between, especially from that "Third Coast" called Texas.

I first issued a call for poems about wine pre-pandemic. I was thinking my way to publish the book and schedule readings at various wineries when the world tilted and was shuttered. I drank a lot of wine at the time, but I shelved the "wine book" and moved on to feel really sorry for myself. It took me a long time, months and months and months actually, to gain momentum, regroup, and contact the list of contributors with updates and promises. Only one gave up on the project and sent a snippy email that she simply couldn't wait any longer. Thank you to everybody else who maintained our connections and exercised extraordinary patience.

The photographs were all obtained from websites specializing in copyright-free images. *Unsplash* and *Pixabay* give photographers a platform to offer their work to the world, and I'm grateful for the opportunity to include the images that magnify the poetry's themes and subjects. I'm the one, with the blessing of the poets, who matched the pictures to their poems. It didn't happen the other way around. In the beginning was the poem, was the word, but the two taken together bridge to a larger metaphor than either one alone.

In addition to the poets and photographers, it took people on the same wave link to turn what began as a vague idea into the finished book. Artist extraordinaire Diana Synatzske painted the watercolor on the cover to perfection, meeting my one request that the cover art not be a wine cliché. Pre-press production guru Jeri Martin and I have worked together for years on various projects, but this time she's also a contributor; slinging type and setting margins aren't her only skills. When I thought about an introduction explaining the history and importance of wine, I immediately thought of Betsy Ball with all her wine credentials. Long-time friends and former colleagues, Betsy and her husband Greg Ball set out on a grand adventure a few years ago. They became nomads and started Euro Travel Coach, a premier travel company. Don't skip the introduction. It provides great insight into our long-standing fascination and love of the grape.

So in spite of being thrown off schedule by months and then by years, I'm pleased to offer *Wine Poems*. Open a bottle of your favorite wine to sip as you read. Savor slowly and enjoy. À votre santé. Beviamo alla nostra. Cheers!

Marilyn Robitaille, Ph.D.

Editor

# Table of Contents

# *Wine Poems*

# Betsy Ball

# Introduction and Invitation

**P**oetry endeavors to stimulate our imagination
and touch our emotions. Wine does the
same. Red or white, sparkling or still, freshly
fermented or aged to perfection, wine stirs our spirit
and moves our soul. Much as poets express their
inner feelings with words, wine inspires us to share
the thoughts that lie hidden beneath our proper
exterior. The Latin phrase *in vino veritas* reveals the
magic of wine, for indeed in wine lies the truth.

Whether we sip alone, drink with friends, or
become more comfortable with strangers as we
indulge in a beautiful glass of wine, when made well
and truly savored, wine is a form of art. What better
way to celebrate all the fermented grape brings to
life than a book of poems and photographs about
wine? This collection is an effort to bring these art
forms together.

I don't know if I can say I am a connoisseur of
wine. That sounds like someone with a wider body
of knowledge than I have acquired to date. That
said, I am truly a wine lover. I have studied wine,
picked and pressed grapes on crisp mornings and
in the hot sun, visited dozens of wineries all over
the world, listened to winemakers talk about their
creations, and had the pleasure of drinking many,
many glasses of wine of countless varieties over
the years. I am not an artist, but I am married to a
musician, so I have also developed a deep love of
art, in many different forms, in the years we have
been together. It is with that bit of background that
I share these thoughts on this unique book of wine
poems.

We know that people have been making wine

for thousands of years. If someone asked you where wine was first made from grapes, what would you say? France? Italy? The cradle of winemaking is Georgia! That's Georgia in Asia, where about 8000 years ago, people learned that if you bury grape juice underground over the winter, it will turn into wine. That alone sounds like magic! By the time of the Greeks around 1000 BC, wine making had become one of the trademarks of Mediterranean civilization.

In Roman times, winemaking became quite sophisticated. Wine was sealed in amphorae with wax. The terracotta vessels were labeled with the year, vineyard, maker and even the type of grape, very much like we label wine today! Interestingly, wine at that time was often mixed with water, and sometimes spices. The one drinking the wine would add their own bit of artistry and season it to taste.

Jesus performed His first miracle by turning water into wine at the wedding of Cana. Even then, it was evident that wine had different levels of quality. In John 2:10 the master of the banquet says, "Everyone brings out the choice wine first and then the cheaper wine after the guests have had too much to drink; but you have saved the best till now." Depending on the party you attend, you could say things haven't changed much to this day.

As Christianity grew throughout Europe, wine became a sacred drink. It symbolized, and with transubstantiation became, the blood of Christ and was a vital element in celebrating Holy Communion. Bishops and monks held an increasingly important role in society as religion became more and more important. Nobility would often give land to the religious orders, and monks would produce the wine needed to celebrate mass. The art of winegrowing can be attributed to the hard work of these monks, who were then also able to sell some of their wines, contributing to the local economy.

Wine was a staple in the medieval Christian diet. In monasteries, monks would often drink wine to the exclusion of water, which would have been unsafe to drink. With the rise of the great European monarchies, the quality of their wine increased. Each abbey and monastery worked to produce the highest quality wine in order to protect their reputation. Wine became important to the local market and to trade, much as it is today in many parts of the world.

The first vineyard and winery in California was established by Catholic missionaries from Spain in 1769. California is now the largest wine producing state in the US. Even though the American wine industry experienced an enormous setback from prohibition, it has since recovered, and the quality of US wine rivals others all over the world.

Wine's importance to history, religion, economics, agriculture, wisdom, and art is unquestioned. It has charmed and blessed us and sometimes cursed us for over eight millennia for good reason. Its magic and appeal are robust and enduring.

Vitis Vinifera is the traditional European grape variety used to make most fine wine. The terroir that produces the best grapes is often rugged, rocky, and subject to all kinds of vulnerabilities that range from birds to badgers and from frost to hail. These grapes only grow between thirty and fifty degrees latitude, north and south of the equator. All the famous regions for wine production around the world are located within these two parallel bands. It is a wonder that grapes can even grow in these limited areas. For them to be harvested and ultimately transformed into the magnificent beverage we pour into a glass is remarkable. When we pair it, and share it at the table, it becomes even more magical.

The enchanted nature of wine is undisputable among wine lovers and those who celebrate by raising a glass. Even those whose lives revolve around wine save the finest bottles for truly special occasions. I remember listening to the great-granddaughter of a major Barolo producer talk about her family's vintages. She told us that we might imagine that they enjoy special bottles every night of the week, and that it's not a big thing for them to have one of their finest bottles any time they feel like it. But in reality, for her family to open a special vintage is a very big deal. She said she had to give birth to a great-great-grandchild in order for her father to go deep in the cellar and find a truly special bottle with which to celebrate!

That same great-granddaughter once invited us to join her in her family's restaurant above their winery on our very first visit to Piedmont. We thought there would be other patrons enjoying the company of the Abbona family, but indeed, it was just our family of four that walked in at 8:00 p.m. sharp to find white tablecloths, multiple enormous, beautiful wine glasses and no one else in the room. We felt quite uncomfortable and out of place.

We sat down with empty glasses and our kind server asked what we would like to taste. We said "everything," and they started us off with a lovely glass each. By the time the Abbonas came to join us, in typical Italian time, we were already enjoying their hospitality and had overcome our insecurities. We had a fantastic evening savoring what their family has worked for five generations to create. You can feel each year's hard labor inside the glass, and their difficult work and deep dedication are reflected in what they have crafted in a labor of love.

# Wine Poems

It is truly magic.

Wine and art go hand in hand. Those who grow grapes and make wine are artists, creating their own form of magic. Some of the most beautiful wineries even surround themselves with other forms of art—from sculpture, to paintings to labels created lovingly and artistically by well-known and lesser-known artists.

Family wineries are sacred places where the owners, through more passion than science, take care to understand the soil, watch the weather, prune what won't benefit the grape, pick with care, press and ferment in sterile containers, blend if desired and then wait—patiently—to see how it all turns out with or without a barrel or multiple years of age.

So, the winery and the terroir are integral, but to truly savor a great wine elevates the human spirit beyond place and passion. The real magic is in savoring the wine and sharing with friends. Wine makes any occasion an opportunity to celebrate the human character and its capabilities.

It seems fitting to collect these poems and photographs about wine so that we can blend these unique art forms in one place, just as Bordeaux blends merlot, cabernet and cabernet franc to make one of the most valuable wines in the world.

Robert Louis Stevenson said, "Wine is bottled poetry." What a perfect reflection of the book you have before you. I recommend that before you sit down to peacefully enjoy *Wine Poems*, pour yourself a glass, and consider the magic contained therein. Even better, after reading some of these contributions, find a friend and fill their glass, too, and discuss the art in the glass and the art between these pages.

Salute!

# Wine Poems

*Pexels Timur*

J .A. Farina

# saving the world

the sun is about to set
as you moor the boat for the night
we've run to Bobcaygeon and back
buying our annual shoes
and carrying boxes heavy with wine
from Niagara, Australia and France—
the table is set for our meal
candles lighting the easy mood
on this north summer night
under skies fragrant with Kawartha pine—
we talk of our past and the young
things we did, lost friends and our children
now grown into men
the plight of those trapped
in the new war abroad—our glasses full
of Australian shiraz,
  we start saving the world—
the answer to all crises
and catastrophes become  clear
as our knowledge increases
to correct global affairs
with every glass
of French Sauvignon,
we start saving the world.
as polaris rises,
  glowing bright overhead
its constellation almost touched
by the pines at the ridge of
this island core—
the boat makes love to the rhythmic waves
as we rise and look out at the moonlit
silent lake—nodding and drained,
after saving the world . . .

J .A. Farina

## Muse

over espressoed and under wined
he daydreams of another night
one that was in another life
his cups full, his mind alert
his muses whispering
sangiovese and rioja dreams
confirming to him now
that wine inspires poetry
caffeine just keeps you awake

J .A. Farina

# vendemma

between the rows of Tuscan vinyards
you can fall back into time
the sun anointing your brow
as it caresses the grapes
the rising scent of earth
and ripened sangiovese, a portal
to an ancient art, a song to
gods of harvest and pressing wine
in rhythm to the seasons
a craft blessed in myth and history
celebrated among the vinyard rows
rooted in vintages and high houses
transcending every barrier
nobility and plebians made equal
their same truth in crystal or ceramic cups
earth and sky and vinyard in each swallow

*Diana Agapova*

Dianne P.Capell

# Mid-Summer Wine

I met my love in a wooded glade
By the bank of a murmuring stream
He kissed my hand as I arrived
With a blanket, tarts, and cream

A silver platter held the crystal carafe
Containing wine of cellar merit
 He filled my glass and then one more
With a ruby- jeweled Claret.

The stone-fruit bouquet stirred my senses
His eyes urged me to taste
Nectar purred over tongue and teeth
There was no need for haste.

We ate and drank as the moon rose high
Pouring glitter on emerald leaves
The wine set free guarded passion
Breathless, I implored, "Please!"

His voice began in a soft baritone
 Cascading in metered verse
A pair of doves cooed a chorus
In this nocturnal universe.

Struggling awake as sunshine warmed
My face from drowsy slumber
I longed for this dream to come again
When daylight turns to umber.

## Dianne P.Capell

# Jazz and Summer Solstice

How did you know that I had
wallowed my way
 into this deep funk

Lamenting the woes of our
broken society
Our sick world-full of hate,
violence,
And mental poverty

How could you know how much
I miss him
His wit, compassion, his love

Why do I have to spend this
 Midsummer alone
Sipping a new wine, listening to
 jazz with its twists and turns

Modulating, undulating,
as the heroine of a Fellini film

The wine is sweet, the music fine
Why not

# Wine Poems

# Wine Poems

*Tim Mossholder*

Paul Moore

# Remember the Vineyards and Bars

Walking in and out of the vines
Picking the fruit from the canes
Biding my time
Before we squash the grapes
Is it a good one or just like all the other years?
Making the wine using blood sweat and tears
Till we can drink it with friends, who say cheers
Losing our inhibitions and losing our fears
People are all different, all sorts of shapes
Sizes and characters, all we can find
Tasting the alcohol, tasting the beers
Tasting the cider and tasting the wine
Have it with cheese and have it with crackers
Mingling with others is one of the factors
Eventually the pub closes when everyone's knackered
In the morning we'll all be fine
Go through the hangover over again
Till the late evening when back on the mend
Drink with a relative drink with a friend
Back to go out to the wine bar again
When will the vicious circle ever end?
Have a Chiante
Have a Rioja or Merlot
Have a Soave
Or Sauvignon Blanc
Have a red wine or Rosé or white
No matter what you're worried about
No matter what you want
Everything is going to be all right
Remember the walking through grapes in the vineyard

## Wine Poems

Picking the fruit from the canes
Remember the waiting, biding our time
Remember the pubs and remember the wine bars
Remember the morning when everything is fine
Remember the drinking with a relative or friend
When will the vicious circle ever end?

# Wine Poems

*Ira Pavlyukovich*

## Hank Jones

# Wine Meditations

I.

The wine glasses touch,
ring like a Buddhist bell
that calls us to prayer.

II.

If there's a sound more
beautiful than wine glasses touching,
it's the sound of a newly opened bottle of wine
glug-glug-glugging into my glass.

III.

Wine viscously circles the bowl of my glass,
leaving legs ZZ Top could sing about.

IV.

The ancient Greeks liked to talk about the
        wine-dark sea.
I like to talk about the sea-dark wine in my glass.

V.

I got drunk once on French wine
under cherry blossoms in Japan,
then drove back to my apartment with a pretty girl.
There's only one part of that I regret.

*Ralph Darabos*

## Eileen R. Tabios

# Smoke Taint

The Times *analyzed every wildfire since 1950, when the California Department of Forestry and Fire Protection began reliably tracking the size and spread of fires. In the last 20 years, more acres have burned in the region than in the entire previous half-century.*
—Los Angeles Times, *Nov. 7, 2019*

October is becoming
synonymous with fire

here in Napa Valley
dedicated to wine.

We met over pinot noir
at Bistro Don Giovanni.

You'd persuaded them
to put your family's tradition

on their wine list. "There."
Your finger pointed

at your label before it rose
to caress my cheek.

I could not anticipate
the morning I would wake,

unable to recall autumn
with the last time I felt

your hand lingering
against my skin. The ash

in my mouth from last
night's dinner pour

reflected "smoke taint,"
you said, "from the latest

California wildfire." All
month, our eyes were

beaten by yellowed skies.
But even fire and smoke

could not camouflage
the true source of

what scorched our
relationship. Still, I nod,

affirm, "Smoke taint."
I don't say anything

about my expertise
in oenology, hard-

earned through other
men not so different

from you. I don't share
how an injured vine

can be salvaged — *saved* —
from fire damage

with proper pruning:
clean cuts to avoid

hurting what remains
healthy enough to survive.

*Wine Poems*

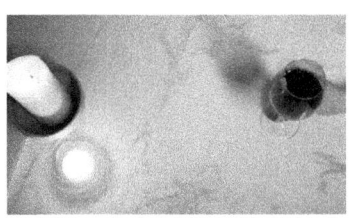

# Wine Poems

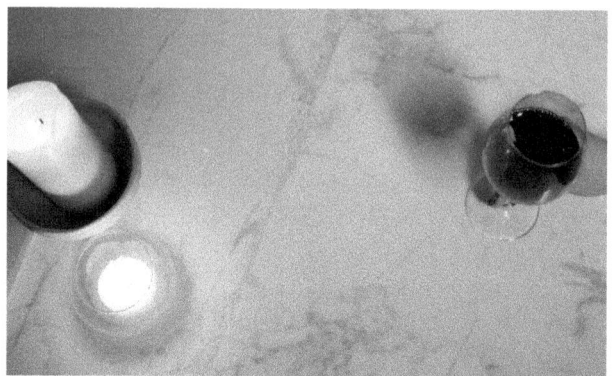

*Artem Podrez*

# Jose Castelleja

## Wine and Memories

In a southern plaza
where the champion mariachis sing

At a coffee table,
we sipped on wine during midday
and watched strangers shop.

A fine love by my side, I'm deeply in love
your lovely eyes and tender heart spark.
The wind waving through your blond and black
    peppered hair,
mesmerized me to the core.

Her blouse and jeans showed a wise, mature lady.
She wore a light perfume that smelled of fresh
honey.
To be a bee in a honey comb.

Her face showed her kind brown eyes,
slender nose and crafty cheeks.
In her eyes I could see the intelligence of time, craft
of thought and attractive smile.

Let me tell you my secret.
A secret you must know.

I was 42 and alone, when i met you.
I was addicted to you.

I was a young vaquero in South Texas,
you might remember.
I was young and without a care,
In this world till I met you.
My heart broke apart
and came together stronger than before.

Jose Castelleja
*(Translation Ivelisse Urbán Hernández)*

# Vino y Recuerdos

En una plaza del sur
donde cantan los mariachis campeones

En un café
tomamos vino durante el día
mientras otros iban de compras.

Un gran amor a mi lado
Estoy bien enamorado
tus hermosos ojos
tu dulce corazón.

Aquellos momentos juntos
gratos fueron
tus sonrisas me intrigaban
y ese día me di cuenta
que estaríamos unidos.

Desde esos tempranos días
te quiero más y más.

Mi amor es incondicional
y sueño cómo juntos
somos la perfección.

Solo el tiempo lo dirá.

# Wine Poems

*Klara Kulikova*

Sandi Horton

# The Wine Glass

I stand on the table in my sparkling, crystal shape
Beckoning a human to fill my insides with wine
I'm tired of being alone and empty

I long for fingers that swirl my insides
And wait for the intimacy of the nose
Drawing out the bouquet of the wine

Then, the gentle lips touch my thin rim
Ever so slowly, sipping a slight sample
I hear the human release a contented sigh

My purpose is being fulfilled with each sip
I inspire conversation and give pleasure
My future is secure

*Eminumana*

# Larry Mayfield

## Inside the Bottle

A knife and fork in hand medium-rare T-bone bake potato salad green bean chow down with a slosh-back of red wine dry aftertaste adorn a table set for one. My thoughts eat through time to an era of American prohibition, the Lost Generation of expatriates wandering abroad and transitioning into a *génération perdue*, captured in a framed picture on my dining-area wall, a bustling come-to-life scene of carefree gaiety at a 1920s quaint sidewalk Parisian café. Chatterbox talk of painters and poet dreamers and wannabe novelists sipping appellation-defined varietals from a plethora of vineyards scattered throughout France, Burgundy to Bordeaux to the Rhône Valley, a Pinot noir or Chardonnay or Syrah, whether it be red white rosé sparkling or blended, dry or sweet. Gather 'round gusto to encounter a bullfight with Ernest and quibble a bit with F. Scott and Zelda while Cole pianos a tune to run skip leap and toss with a barefoot Isadora clad in scarf hanging in ambiguity around an abstract of Pablo depicting the allure of Josephine in mid-legacy performance at the Folies Bergère. And I ponder, did Gertrude's quote mean a rose is a rose...or a rosé?

Retire to the den with a second glass full of fermenting flavor to take the edge off, pouring over affections of my lover of choice. Swirl around, inhale aroma, sip, a taste of lip-to-lip drip, spirited pheromones still linger. Musical interlude, listen to Sir Elton's, "Hold me closer, Tiny Dancer," wishful to embrace you, my love, baring our souls, our shortcomings, and just sit back mind-buzzing with needle in groove, Nina playing-out my relatable life, "Ain't Got No - I Got Life," my out-of-tune voice warbling out of harmony. Even though I don't got money culture friends or no gods . . . I got brains heart soul life and my freedom. My songs of innocence lost out to experiencing the value of having loved. Nearing the end of the second glass, my altered state of mind falls into an entranced meditation where I see and think nothing consciously, yet unconsciously there is likely a balance. The music could still be playing, the heart could still be loving, the wine could still be sipped. When empty, refill, the symbology of that glass filling/emptying/filling, and of a life once full that became empty, to hopefully fill yet again.

৪০

An unassuming glass number three to mull over what haunts me. Down into the depths of mindful complexity, a stare-down risking seventeen years of sobriety unraveling, tip-toeing the line. Uncorking all those battles with alcohol, attending AA meetings, gaining weapons to combat the addiction, a knife cutting to the chase, finding old war stories of drinking stored away in a bottle. Joining in again and again at a yearly-tradition Christmas party with friends gathered, a clink of glass toasting to good health, honor, happiness. Colorful red and green garland decorations coming down, and a conical-shaped conifer discarded. The habitual weekly grind resumes, a return to banal monotony, senses dulled, laughter fading. Awareness of an unforgotten love lying inside a bottle, a flashback of stains resembling spilled wine remaining soiled, songs skipping a beat repeatedly, and the smoke of snuffed-out cigarettes still hovers, fouling the air. What was once a realism

painting of my life, those gentle warming panoramic
sunrise hues cloud-over by midday, a whipping
blue norther blowing my calm into chaos, and
behind those ever-changing faces of the past within
the clouds, abstract chilled icicles and nightfall
prohibit the swallow of recovery.

&

Peering through the thick bottle darkening, a
deliberate pour of last glass four, topsy-turvy
bottom-of-the-bottle dregs. Fill to the brim, suckle
off the top, seemingly above the rim, careful as to
not spill another drop. Bring to mind and salute
a dear friend I drank with heavily on countless
occasions. Sitting back against a dumpster, hump-
backed stupor, head down, bottle in hand, dead . .
. his familiar chuckle ceased. A last breath tainted
with the scent of wine, as I slink over onto my couch
toppled, head on pillow, a California Cabernet
Sauvignon emptied out, sleeping in dreams of
drunken never-ending travels inside a bottle.

# Wine Poems

Roland Dumke

# Ray Diamond

## To Come

I lived as near as dammit in a vineyard
For three months of my life, regular and stunted
The vines I walked between. One dog on a leash
One free to roam, to enjoy the harvest
Left over from the previous year. I was
"House-sitting," more a gite, really, for an American
Who lived in two halves of the globe,
Here for the sun, the picking, the company
Of transient workers, away when winds were cold.

It was March. I say, I got frost-bite from a snowstorm,
Unseasonal, they assured me, read Verlaine
And Rimbaud when the sun was shining,
Walked in woods with traps and baying dogs,
Faintly medieval, probably unwise.
And now when I drink wine I think of slopes
Bare and sinister in the failing light,
The plants like wood, but with all that sunshine
Locked in the grain, ready to burst out.

*Maria Orlova*

Tom Murphy

# The Island of Jupiter

On the Bordeaux peninsula, we had stopped in Bordeaux properly, driven from San Sebastián, sitting outside of Saint Michel to figure our route on the newly acquired wine map, slowly driving north along the Garonne and decided to stop at Château Lynch-Bages. A fine Pauillac that we tasted in their stately château many different vintages of clarets. Leisurely, we meandered west to Benon and sought our night's stop. Le Bled campsite where old refrigerators were on their backside with doors removed for planter boxes; bean and tomato cages and lavender grew — cacti in toilets dot our garden now, was a bare-bones campsite, with a picnic table, a WC with shower, but no fire ring.

On our way to Pointe de Grave for the car ferry across Garonne to Royan and Chenonceau, we wanted to visit an artesian winery — a smaller château, more local and less industrial. The map listed Château Laulan Ducos in the Medoc appellation, a little out of our direction. The owner, Francis Ducos, didn't speak English, although nice, alone, with no tasting room. Susan talked with the Vigneron in broken French and he was glad to share his laborious wines. We bought a bottle of each 1990 and 1991 vintages of his Insula Jovis — The Island of Jupiter. We hauled those bottles across Europe and home in the states and laid them down to age. That day with Mr. Ducos in his cluttered château as he worked hard to doll out his wares a sweet memory aroused with each cork popping, decanting and tasting years later.

Later, Château Laulan Ducos was purchased in 2011 by Richard Shen, the actor Shen Dongjun of

## *Wine Poems*

the Chinese Jewelry chain store TESiRO, now called
Leysen that has four hundred stores, where bottles
of Insula Jovis will be sold, using the face of actress
Zhang Ziyi of *The Wasted Times.*

> centuries old vines
> Medoc artesian claret
> honeymoon palate

# Wine Poems

*Posawee Suwannaphati*

## Beatrice Fernandez

# Anticipation

The sounds that form
the notes of your name
spoken in a stranger's voice,
or the glint of wine-red hair
under the foyer chandelier —
and my glass in nervous fingers
swirls its contents to the brim,
tilts and spills, overflows —
burgundy drops trembling on the rim,
the way a first-time diver
hesitates on the precipice,
fearing the fiery sting
of that radiant ringing surface.

With a deep breath I brace
against the cacophony
of my heartbeat
I stare down into what's left
in my rotund glass
dark mauve lees
shape-shifting like tea leaves
in a gypsy's cup

Right now, I don't need
all possible fortunes foretold
because I know —
poison or cure,
I want to take it all in,
savor it sip by sip,
down to the forbidden dregs —
serve it to the perfect prison
of my two lips.

*Ilya Gorborukov*

Teresa Roberson

# Dear Malbec

Like fine wine
My tastes
Improved over time
My childhood favorites
Whole milk and sugary Kool-Aid
Both outgrown

The roaring twenties
Punctuated with
White-wine spritzers
Girly cocktails
Sugary shots
Sipped to savor

The flirty thirties
Chicly sipping red wine
The drier the better
And voluptuous like me
My favorite pairing?
With spicy dark chocolate

The phenomenal forties
Introduced to Malbec
During an introductory
Tango class
The classes ended
The Malbec didn't

Red wine's
Heart healthy
A delicious
Daily supplement
Meditation in a glass
Om

# Wine Poems

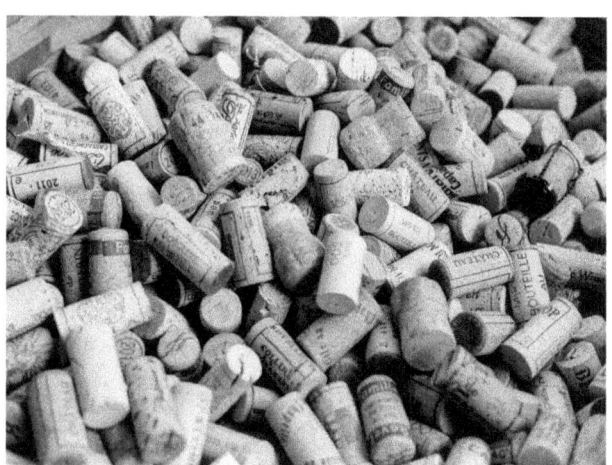

Elisha Terada

# Zee Mink-Fuller

# I Wanted to Shove a Cork Up His Nose

The years spanned indistinctly between my high school
sweetheart and my middle aged self
Divorce ripped apart love with infidelity and
desertion while still fresh from the alter
Abandonment was a foreign notion to my naive hippie
flower child heart

I learned to turn broken promises into freedom
Raising a baby alone, working for food and electricity,
made for a strong willed spirit

Years later the idle wanderer resurfaced, asking for
    entrance
into my daughter's life
She, hungry for a father's touch, agreed with the
    naivety her
mother once wore

She asked for my quiet assistance and support at their
    dinner
meeting, I agreed, hoping I could leave bitterness at
    the door
—I was unsuccessful

Her sperm donor father brought friends for support
These friends were vulgar, rich wine snobs, who
    uncorked a
bottle of merlot with the flare of Robert Parker, Jr
—without the cred

My old flame (I saw only a pile of cold ashes) asked
    for the
sommelier to present yet another expensive wine to be
uncorked

# Wine Poems

He, knowing my tee totaling ways, made a dramatic
    play pouring
me a glass of the dark red after passing the cork
under his out of joint nose

My daughter gave me "the look" . . . too late, my hand
    was in the air
motioning for the maitre d'
The tux clad somber fellow, asked what he could do
    for me
In a clear, albeit dripping with sarcasm voice, I asked
for a glass of 7 Up

All eyes beaded in on my blasphemous hand pouring
    a two dollar
glass of soda into a forty dollar glass of wine,
I then, sipped my concoction with a big smile on my
    satisfied lips

Soon after, the fornicating snake slithered away, never
    to surface again
It wasn't my uncouth treatment of the grape harvest
    which made
for his quick retreat,
it was his depraved self—incapable of unconditional
love,
although he did look comically dashing with the cork I
visualized up his nose

My daughter, flourished in spite of her paternal
    genetics,
I learned to enjoy drinking sweet garnet fluid from
    a box
with other strong willed middle-aged women while
    sitting
around a conversation stained table

## Wine Poems

Mathilda Langevin

Betsy Joseph

# A Flute Too Far

You have done it again, mon cheri,
your hand on my knee in the car.
The first flute of bubbly certainly charmed me—
The fourth glass, a flute too far.

The flattery, attention, the winsome smile—
you have done it again, mon cheri.
And well into that smooth first mile,
the first flute of bubbly certainly charmed me.

You have done it again, mon cheri
with your forthright and debonair way.
The first flute of bubbly certainly charmed me;
I so enjoyed the first act of the play.

With your forthright and debonair way,
you certainly have honed your routine.
I so enjoyed the first act of the play—
my recall less clear of the last scene.

You certainly have honed your routine—
your hand on my knee in the car.
My recall less clear of the last scene,
the fourth glass, a flute too far.

# Wine Poems

*Igor Starkov*

# Rene Ornes

# A Beaujolais to Remember

Lost in thought sitting at a beach side bar in Cabo,
watching moonlight dancing across the waves,
while listening to the surf crashing on the shore,
I sipped from a tall wine glass, half full of a chilled,
friendly and comfortable Pinot Gregio.
Singing ballads, playing guitar was a not so young man,
unshaven, well-worn clothes and a deep base voice.
I could only speculate, why Cabo and why this bar?
The cool evening breeze changed and it now
carried the scent of freshly cut gardenias.
She sat only two bar stools away and smiled.
Raising my glass of Pinot, I returned her smile.
After a few minutes, she put her wine list down
and leaning toward me requested a recommendation.
"I must ask you first some questions, madam.
Are you feeling light and sparkling or perhaps sweet
and delicate, maybe serious, dry and to the point?"
She gave it thought, then rolled her big green eyes,
"I prefer a red, but nothing serious or too dry,
playful but not bubbly, delicate nor too sweet."
"Alfredo, a glass of Beaujolais for the lady."
The conversation was superficial, but flowed
until my phone rang; it was my wife.
I excused myself, but was back only minutes later.
Her bar stool now sat empty; she was on the beach.
Turning back, she smiled and slowly walked away.
I didn't follow; instead, I said goodbye to Beaujolais
and took another sip of Pinot, my old friend.

# Wine Poems

*Markus Spiske*

## Gail Tyson

## Over There

No foot locker could hold the tank
he drove across bodies, or muscle-
throbbing gunfire, or his youth left
over there with Spam, Lucky Strikes.

Tucked in the Belgian linen shipped
home, heirloom nightmares still blinding
white decades later, still ruby
treacle like that bottle of Bordeaux
bought V-E Day, the one he never
opened.

*Andrew Neel*

Jeri D. Martin

# A Boxed Set

Rainy afternoon
boxed wine
and you.

Washing the car
in the rain
and you.

My first taste of wine
and love
and you.

Napa wineries
offer variety
and amazing landscapes.

No boxed wine in Napa
no love
and no you.

*Roman Odintsov*

# Lydia Elizabeth Percy

## Submittable Portal to Wine

A whirring Rolling Stones
Sister morphine at the end stylus skid
Bottle of red wine; two
Lavender pills ready to mouth mix
Eyelids flip flap lock over to a snooze
Listening  "Boweavil Blues"
Blends between Mama's old phonograph record
crackle
Warp record undulating on turns fade
After the shade shut the suns light out
Bottle of red Fat Bastard gone . . .
All that could be heard was the last record
Arm drop click to begining
Ticking around to the sound of BJ's Captain Jack
Pop another bottle of Fat Bastard.

Batuhan Kocabas

## Natalie Inzero Ayala

# Taste My Quarantine

I'm sitting here in the dark surrounded by my
    memories,
Alone and afraid it's hard to even breathe.
I pick up my friend so sweet and so plush,
My lips and my tongue anticipate the rush.
Slowly the taste brings me back to crowds and cheer,
Will I ever be able to drink my wine without fear.

*Picha*

## Suzanne Cate

# Golden

My love and I, seeking some beauty,
Sat outside in our lawn chairs
to bask in the glow of the full, golden March moon.
We lifted our glasses of chilled Chardonnay
In a toast to the shimmering sphere shining back at us,
Wine magnifying the moonlight.
The mild March breeze complimented the glow
of moon and mellow wine as we sat and sipped and
    gazed quietly,
letting moon and wine suffuse us with peace.
As each gently worked its magic upon us and within us
I breathed a sigh of gratitude for the near fifty years
that have mellowed us for this moment.
Golden glow of wine, golden glow of moon,
Golden anniversary.
Gifts of the universe to grace us.

# Wine Poems

*Laura Stanley*

## T. Wayne Schwertner

They call it terroir.
A subtle essence
of land
and water.
Scientists will say
it's all chemistry —
interplay of elements,
roots,
fruit.

It's more.
A dance
between wine and memory.
Washing over the tongue
gently awakening the past.
A snippet of song.
The laughter in her eyes.
Crispness of the air.
A hint of woodsmoke
lingering.
Wine and mind touching
as lovers touch fingertips.

# Wine Poems

*Jill Burrow*

# Moumin Quazi

## *In Remembrance of Me*

*"In the same way, after supper He took the cup, saying,
'This cup is the new covenant in My blood; do this,
whenever you drink it, in remembrance of Me.'"*
(The First Epistle of Paul to the Church in Corinth,
11:25)

Sleep is a strange thing,
The place of sought-after liminality,
Of inbetween-ness,
Straddling the here and the there
Where I know but don't know,
Where I remember but only in pieces.
A short hibernation.
A miniature death.
Wine takes me there,
And I am present only there.
And when I am back here,
I only remember in pieces,
Before what I have known so surely
Is gone again,
And almost certainly never existed.
You are like that.
Were you ever there?
Did I ever know you?
It seemed so.
How can I believe
When only my name means, "Believer"?
You said to remember you when I drink it,
But how can I do that when I can hardly
Recall that time we once ate?
Did I dream that supper?
Did I make up that sacrifice?
The bread? The breaking?

## Wine Poems

The pouring out? The drinking?
Or was it just a story I read?
About the first of the four
Dionysian rituals,
The slaughter of the piglets,
Before the actors take the stage,
And I reawaken.

# Contributors

**Natalie Ayala**  Natalie Ayala has a passion for the arts. She's a raging artist, creative in abstract painting, writing, photography, and floral design. Natalie was born and raised in West Haven, Connecticut. She's a mother of three and a grandmother of five. Family is very important to her, so much so that she helped deliver four out of the five grandchildren. Post COVID, Natalie focuses more on her painting, but every once in a while, she'll still pick up a pen and start writing. As a matter of fact she's just started writing a book.

**Betsy Ball**  Betsy Ball is co-founder and partner of Euro Travel Coach (ETC), which crafts custom European vacations for independent travelers and leads small group trips to Europe. She is a passionate and culturally curious traveler who thoroughly enjoys sharing her love for exploring Europe with ETC clients. Prior to founding ETC, Betsy taught International Business at Tarleton State University in Texas (part of the A & M System) where she led study abroad trips to multiple European countries and other worldwide destinations. She retired from teaching five years ago and now lives in Madison, Wisconsin, spends summers at her cottage in Quebec,

# Wine Poems

and travels several months of the
year in Europe. She has a degree
in hotel, restaurant management
from Michigan State University and
an MBA from Southern Methodist
University in Dallas. She also holds a
Level 3 certification from the Wine &
Spirits Education Trust.

**Dianne Capell**  Dianne was born and
raised in Pampa, a small town in the
Texas Panhandle, where she was first
inspired by stories of the indigenous
and colonial histories of the area.
Frequent visits to Palo Duro Canyon
and Panhandle Plains Historical
Museum in Canyon were anticipated
with great delight. After graduating
from Baylor University (BME) and
West Texas State University (MM),
she pursued her life-long ambition of
being a music educator. This pursuit
took her to Texas City, Dallas, and
ultimately overseas to teach in the
Department of Defense Dependent
Schools in Sasebo and Yokosuka,
Japan and finally, Naples, Italy. After
twenty years overseas Dianne and
her family returned to the Panhandle
to retire.  While overseas, Dianne
began writing poetry highlighting
journeys through Japan and Italy.
Dianne especially likes to write in
the poetic forms, Haiku, sonnet, ode,
couplets, and lyric.  Her recent poetic
expressions are found in free verse.
Dianne's poem in this collection is
expressed in the lyric form.

## Wine Poems

**Jose R. Castilleja**   Jose R. Castilleja is a writer, a poet, an engineer, and community leader. He has written articles of events, poems for journals and the local newspaper in Alamo, Texas. He was born and raised in the Rio Grande Valley and has worked in Texas and California.

**Suzanne Cate**   Suzanne Cate is happily retired after more than thirty years in local church music ministry, most recently at Acton UMC. She and husband Michael, formerly a teacher and  assistant principal at Acton Middle School, have moved to Shreveport, Louisiana, to be near their son, daughter-in-law and grandgirls. They stay very busy downsizing their stuff and upgrading their backyard. Most late afternoons you'll find them on their patio sipping a glass o' red and giving thanks for the blessing of fifty-two years together!

**Ray Diamond**   Ray Diamond is a poet and performer based in London, England. He is the author of three full books of verse with reputable publishers, as well as a full-length play. A fourth volume is due out this autumn. His work has appeared in many magazines, including *South Bank Poetry* and *The Interpreter's House*.

# Wine Poems

**Joseph A Farina**  Joseph A Farina, an internationally award-winning poet, is a retired lawyer in Sarnia, Ontario, Canada. Several of his poems have been published in *Quills, Canadian Poetry Magazine, The Wild Word, The Chamber Magazine, Lothlorian Poetry Journal, Ascent, Subterranean Blue,* and in *The Tower Poetry Magazine, Inscribed, The Windsor Review,* and *Boxcar Poetry Revue.* His work also appears in many anthologies including: *Sweet Lemons: Writings with a Sicilian Accent; Canadian Italians at Table; Witness from* Serengeti Press; and *Tamaracks: Canadian Poetry for the 21st Century.* He has had poems published in U.S. magazines including *Mobius, Pyramid Arts, Arabesques, Fiele-Festa, Philadelphia Poets* and *Memoir.* He has had two books of poetry published: *The Cancer Chronicles* and *The Ghosts of Water Street.*

**Beatriz F. Fernandez**  Beatriz F. Fernandez is the author of *Shining from a Different Firmament* (Finishing Line Press, 2015) which was featured at the Miami Book Fair International and *The Ocean Between Us* (Backbone Press, 2017). She's a *Writer's Digest* Poetry Award Grand Prize winner and three-time *Pushcart* nominee; her recent work appears in *Prime Number Magazine, Mom Egg Review* and *Whale Road Review.* Twitter handle @nebula61, IG: nebula4291, www.beasbooks. blogspot.com

## Wine Poems

**Sandi Horton**   Sandi Horton completed a B.M.E. (music) from Texas Tech University and a M.S. (Ed Psy) from Baylor University. She performed original music compositions on two solo CD albums: *Native Flute Journeys* released in June 2018 and *Native Flute Journeys* 2 released in March 2020. Her music has been featured on One World Radio several times. In July 2021, Sandi attended and performed at a native flute retreat led by R. Carlos Nakai in Montana. In March 2019, she performed her native flute music and poetry at the Art & Psyche International Conference in Santa Barbara, California. She was the 2018 *Langdon Review* Writer-in-Residence. She has three books of published poetry *My House of Poetry* (2014), *Where is Yonder?* (2017), and *Restore Thyself* (2018).  Sandi has been the chairperson  of the Waco WordFest and editor of the *WordFest Anthology* 2016-2021. She worked in public schools as a band director and school counselor for nineteen years. She and her husband Jeff have two grown children, two granddaughters, and a houseful of rescue dogs.

## Wine Poems

**Hank Jones**  Hank Jones backpacked the world in his youth hoping to find a poet within until lack of funds prompted him to seek a job at his alma mater, Tarleton State University. He planned to stay a year or two and get back on the road, but twenty-one years later, he is an assistant professor at the same university. To keep his creative spirit alive, and to hone his facility with the written word, he enrolled in the Red Earth MFA program at Oklahoma City University from which he graduated in 2019. His first book of poetry, *Too Late for Manly Hands*, was published by Turning Plow Press in 2021. He now lives in a beautiful house overlooking Lake Keystone with his wife and a clowder of cats and drives six hours to teach his courses at Tarleton.

**Betsy Joseph**  Betsy Joseph, a retired English professor, lives in Dallas and has poems which have appeared in a number of journals and anthologies. Her poetry collection, *Only So Many Autumns,* was published by Lamar University Literary Press in 2019.  Lamar is also publishing her forthcoming book, *Relatively Speaking: Poems of Person and Place,* a collaborative collection of poetry with her brother and poet Chip Dameron.

# Wine Poems

**Jeri D. Martin**   Jeri D. Martin, a Native Texan, spent some time exploring the world before returning to her home state. After twenty-five years working as a graphic designer, she decided to go to school to become an English instructor. Now in her seventh year teaching English, and she still thinks it might be a dream. Since third grade, writing short stories and poetry about personal adventures has been a creative outlet. She now lives in Stephenville, Texas, with Blue and T-Bone, her two rescue dogs.

**Larry Mayfield**   An inveterate folklore and nature enthusiast, native Texan Larry Mayfield gained interest in the environment early on. After his formative schooldays and studies at Tarleton State University, an appetite for connection to his locale took him to serve on boards of the Western Cross Timbers Archaeological Assoc., Erath County Horticulture Assoc., and Stephenville Historical House Museum, wherein he organized the annual Native and Heirloom Plant Fair. Mayfield, a retired postal carrier and singer/songwriter, published a song "You Gotta Believe" in 2005 through Hungry for Music and a Native-style song, "Grandfather's Spirit," recorded on Red Feather Woman's award-winning CD, *Keeper of the Dreams*, in 2013. In 2015, he authored *A Whisper's Shadow Apart* (autobiographical journal with self-penned music CD) followed

# Wine Poems

by *Tributaries and Stepping Stones* (poetry/poetic prose/spoken word) in 2019, both published by Approach the Drum Press. Mayfield and his four-legged companion, Ki-ti, currently reside in Stephenville, Texas.

**Zee Mink-Fuller**  Zee Mink-Fuller writes from rural acreage in Texas, which offers much fodder for her creative imagination. She has been published in a variety of journals, anthologies, magazines, calendars, newspapers, a book of essays and theatre presentations. When not writing or traveling, she dabbles in found art, creating characters from found objects such as wood, glass and metal. She is currently working on a poetry book as well as a book of short stories.

**Paul Moore**  Paul Moore is a London poet whose works have been shared at the Poetry Cafe, Betterton Street, London, England, at various readings over the years. He is a member of the UK Poetry Society.

# Wine Poems

**Tom Murphy**   Tom Murphy is the 2021-2022 Corpus Christi, Poet Laureate and the *Langdon Review*'s 2022 Writer-In-Residence. Murphy's books & CDs: *Snake Woman Moon* (El Grito del Lobo Press, 2021 *forthcoming*), *Pearl* (FlowerSong Press, 2020), *American History* (Slough Press, 2017), co-edited *Stone Renga* (Tail Feather Press, 2017), chapbook, *Horizon to Horizon* (Strike Syndicate, 2015), CDs "Live from Del Mar College" and "Slams from the Pit" (BOW Productions, 2015, 2014). Murphy is a committee member of the Corpus Christi People's Poetry Festival. He teaches at Texas A&M University—Corpus Christi.

**Rene Ornes MD**   Rene is a native Texan, married forty-six years, father of three, grandfather of five. He's retired from medical practice after forty-one years. He developed his artistic side, which had never previously seen the light of day. He now enjoys writing poetry, has written and directed several plays for community theater, and just finished a book. Golf is his addiction, but he also enjoys singing, Tai Chi, traveling, or drinking a glass of wine, watching sunset on the beach with his wife.

# Wine Poems

**Lydia Elizabeth Percy**  Lydia Elizabeth Percy is an American poet from Queens, New York. She is the 1987 recipient of the Literary Achievement Award; winner of the Ntozake Shange Poets Award for her adaptation on the Black Experience, featured poem "Ladies Room," Burrell publisher; and member of NWU/UAW, Local 1981/AFL-CIO. For three decades, she has been an active member of the New York writing community on the Lower East Side Village. As a member and participant, she frequents open readings at: The Inspired Word, St Mark's Poetry Project, Rome Neal's Nyrorican Poets Café, and The Bowery Poets Café. She is a published author of a full volume of poetry titled *Pussy Toes* (published by I Universe). She has completed four volumes of poetry currently in the editing phase: Volume 1 *Trini*; Volume 2 *Call me Atlanta Lockheart*; Volume 3 *Embryo*; Volume 4 *L.I.V.E.* Percy's influences and personal acquaintances include James Baldwin, Rome Neal, Sonia Sanchez, and Amiri Baraka.

# Wine Poems

**Moumin Quazi**  Moumin Quazi is Professor of English at Tarleton State University; the nineteen-year editor of *CCTE Studies*; edits the book series "South Asian Literature, Art, and Culture Studies" (Peter Lang Publishers); the treasurer of the Texas Association of Creative Writing Teachers; founded Scheherazade Press in 2019; has co-edited the *Langdon Review* for fourteen years; and has been widely published. His *Migratory Words* was published by Lamar University Literary Press (2016). He's a really light drinker. His name really does mean "devout faith in Allah," or "Believer."

Winery info:
Llano Estacado Winery
3426 East F.M. 1585
Lubbock, TX  79404

https://llanowine.com

Llano Estacado Sweet Red
(any year)

The reason for my choice of favorite winery and wine is very personal. I enjoyed a wine-tasting there once with a dear friend. I had never done that before, and I got very drunk. It was one of the best days I can barely remember.

# Wine Poems

**Teresa Y. Roberson**  International Math/Science teacher (1992-2014), author, illustrator, podcaster and producer of The Austin Writers Roulette (2012-2019), Teresa Y. Roberson manifests her creative projects through books, blogs and digital and material canvases.

Favorite Winery: Although I've never visited, Cabenero Vineyards would be my choice of vineyard destinations since I love their Red Cabernero. It's my go-to specialty wine for special occasions, thanks to its deliciously bold blend of Cabernet and habarnero peppers.

**T. Wayne Schwertner**  T. Wayne Schwertner is a wildlife conservationist and traveler, a story teller and lover of life, a native Texan and citizen of the Earth.  He grew up in the Texas Hill Country where he developed a deep connection to the land early in childhood, and that connection has been a powerful part of his life ever since.  He has worked and played all over the world, leaving a little bit of his heart everywhere he has gone while taking a little bit of those places with him – and always stopping to have a glass of wine along the way. Whether drinking a glass at dinner in a London restaurant or from a tin cup in a tent surrounded by elephants, wine has been a constant in his travels. His poem "The Dance" was inspired by the deep physical and spiritual connection all people have with the Earth – a connection often manifested through the magic of wine.

**Eileen R. Tabios**   Eileen R. Tabios has released over sixty collections of poetry, fiction, essays, and experimental biographies from publishers in ten countries and cyberspace. In 2022 she releases the poetry collection *Because I Love You, I Become War*; a book-length essay *Kapwa's Novels*; and her second French book, *Double Take* (trans. Fanny Garin). Her 2021 books include her first novel *DoveLion: A Fairy Tale for Our Times* and first French book *La Vie erotique de l'art* (trans. Samuel Rochery). Her award-winning body of work includes invention of the hay(na)ku, a 21st century diasporic poetic form, and the MDR Poetry Generator that can create poems totaling theoretical infinity, as well as a first poetry book, *Beyond Life Sentences*, which received the Philippines' National Book Award for Poetry. Her writing and editing works have received recognition through awards, grants and residencies. More information is at http://eileenrtabios.com

# Wine Poems

**Gail Tyson** In 2020 Shanti Arts published Gail Tyson's chapbook, *The Vermeer Tales*. Tennessee Mountain Writers, Inc. awarded her the 2021 Patricia Boatner Fiction Award Honorable Mention for her short story, "Surely Mercy." An alumna of Stanford's Creative Writing Program and the Dylan Thomas Summer School at the University of Wales, she recently moved to Knoxville, Tennessee, where she serves on the board of Flying Anvil Theatre.

Favorite vineyard name: Sones cellars. Tasting room is at 334-B Ingalls Street, Santa Cruz, CA 95060, blocks from the spectacular West Cliff walk where you can watch surfers. Since 2003, Sones Cellars has focused on Petite Syrah and Zinfandels, producing small lots, and offering Hedgehog White and Red blends in refillable bottles.

Website: sonescellars.com

My favorite wine selection: any Petite Syrah. The 2015 won a gold medal at the *San Francisco Chronicle* wine competition.

## Wine Poems

**Ivelisse Urbán Hernandez**  Ivelisse Urbán Hernández was born and raised in San Juan, Puerto Rico and often tells her students that poetry saves lives. During her years in New York City, in the nineties, she started writing poetry in English. She then switched to writing poetry in Spanish, has been writing in Spanish since, and published a book of poetry in Spain: *Mi cuerpo tus Indias*, DosSoles, 2015. She has a second manuscript that she is hoping to publish soon. She teaches Spanish language and literature at Tarleton State University in Texas (part of the A & M System).

# *Wine Poems*

**Diana Synatzske, Cover Art** Diana Synatzske graduated from Tarleton State University with a BA in art and a secondary teaching certification. During her time in secondary education, she obtained a Masters of Art Education degree from Texas Tech University. After graduating from Texas Tech, she pursued a Master of Fine Arts at Louisiana Tech University and graduated with an MFA in 3D Studio. Diana's work focuses on the discourse and the unexplained lapses in memory from her childhood disclosing a certain amount of anxiety and comfort from aloneness, forming unique dialogs through the medium of clay. Diana owns and operates Curly Tail Panther Studio in Stephenville, Texas, and is currently a visiting professor at Tarleton State University where she teaches multiple studios, art history, and art education courses.

## Wine Poems

**Marilyn Robitaille, Editor**
Marilyn Robitaille recently transitioned from Tarleton State University after a forty-year career teaching English and administering international and study abroad programs. She founded Romar Press, an independent small press, with plans to focus on memoirs through sponsored creativity retreats and workshops. The first one will be held in Vermont in 2023. She has published one book of illustrated poetry *Not by Design: Fifty Poems and Images*, and her work has been included in multiple poetry anthologies and collections. Her poetry appears in the online publication Texas Poetry Assignment, a forum that supports anti-hunger efforts in Texas. She most recently collected, edited, and published *Wine Poems*, a collection of poems and related photographs all extolling the virtues and emotional associations we have wine. She co-founded *Langdon Review of the Arts* in Texas and co-hosted the long-running *Langdon Review* Weekend, a festival of the arts in Granbury, Texas. As a member of the Texas Association of Creative Writing Teachers, she was co-editor and helped found *Writing Texas*, a publication of the Association. She has recently been named Managing Director of the Frazier Conservatory (opening in 2023), a planned private retreat in Stephenville, Texas, that will give special priority to non-profit organizations or events that celebrate the land,

revitalization, the arts, and regional culture. She lives on a ranch with husband Charles Robitaille. Her pride and joy are two grown children Marlow and Chaz, their spouses Brandon and Lauren, and four near-perfect grandchildren Bowen, Ella, Lily, and Crossin.

*Wine Poems*

# Index

# Wine Poems

## *Wine Poems*